GENERATION ENERGY

Paul Mason

Illustrated by **Sophie Scarlett Chadwick**

OXFORD
UNIVERSITY PRESS

Contents

Dear Agent U,

Welcome to Energy Force – a new, worldwide agency dedicated to saving the planet. This is your training manual.

The world is in a serious situation. Our current sources of energy are running out. At the same time, the way we use energy is damaging Earth's environment. We need to find more sources of **sustainable energy** to ensure that we can meet our own energy needs and that future generations can meet theirs.

Energy Force can help to solve the world's energy problems. You don't have to be asked to join: if you want to help, consider yourself a member. Try to recruit others, too. The problems are too substantial for one country to sort out alone, so agents all around the world need to collaborate, looking at the difficulties caused by our current energy sources and attempting to find alternatives.

Your key task is to help people understand that this situation cannot continue, and to suggest how we might change the way we use energy. The good news is that there's still an opportunity to save the planet – but we may not have much time left!

Yours sincerely,

On behalf of Energy Force

INTRODUCTION

This training manual does three important jobs. It:

- *tells* you about the problems caused by our current sources of energy
- *outlines* alternatives that are being developed
- *shows* how we can use less energy in our day-to-day lives.

Who needs energy anyway?

Everyone needs energy for almost everything. Whenever you turn on a light, boost the heating or refrigerate your food, it requires energy.

How it works: Fracking

Fracking is short for 'hydraulic fracturing'. It is a way of extracting gas and oil from rock. A hole is drilled into the earth, then water, sand and chemicals are forced in. This pushes out oil or gas contained in the rock.

So what is the problem?

We are using increasing amounts of energy each year. The world's population is growing, so more people need energy. In addition, a greater number of people live energy-hungry lifestyles. This demand for energy is actually causing *two* problems:

1. The energy sources we currently use – oil, coal and natural gas (the fossil fuels) – are running out.
2. Using fossil fuels is causing damage to our environment.

And what is the solution?

To solve these problems, we need to:

- use less energy
- find energy sources that do not run out or ruin the environment
- think about the future *now*.

This is known as developing a 'sustainable energy strategy'.

Debate this! Fracking

For:

- Fracking keeps energy relatively inexpensive.
- It can be done where few people live.
- Many benefit from the energy produced.

Against:

- Fracking uses huge amounts of water, which is a precious resource.
- It releases chemicals that could cause cancer.
- People fear it may cause small earthquakes.

A brief history of making things work

Humans have been on Earth for tens of thousands of years and, for most of them, we have been using all sorts of energy to get things done.

998 000 BCE Humans living in the Wonderwerk Cave in South Africa learn to burn wood and use fire as a source of heat and light.

300–100 BCE Engineers in ancient Greece develop the waterwheel. The flow of rivers is **harnessed** as a source of power. Waterwheels are also used for irrigation.

100 CE Hero of Alexandria invents the first known wind-powered machine; surprisingly, it is a musical organ!

700–1000 CE In Sistan, part of modern-day Iran, the first windmills are invented. They are made of several sails around the outside of a **vertical axis**, and are used for grinding crops and pumping water.

1600–1700 CE In Britain, engineers discover how to turn coal into coke, a fuel that burns at an extremely high temperature, giving out lots of energy quickly.

1700s CE Engineers develop systems for pumping mines free of water, making it possible to mine coal deep underground. Coal starts to become the main energy source in industrialized countries.

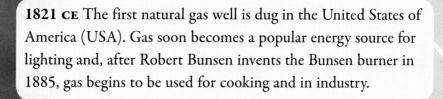

1821 CE The first natural gas well is dug in the United States of America (USA). Gas soon becomes a popular energy source for lighting and, after Robert Bunsen invents the Bunsen burner in 1885, gas begins to be used for cooking and in industry.

1830s CE Electric **generators**, motors and relays are developed, making electricity a possible source of energy.

1858/9 CE The first modern oil well is sunk, in Titusville, USA. During the 1800s, most of the world's oil comes from Russia. After 1900, first the USA and then the Middle East begin to supply more of the world's oil.

1860 CE Auguste Mouchout of France uses the power of the sun (solar energy) to produce steam for the first time.

1880–1900 CE Nikola Tesla and Thomas Edison battle it out to become kings of the new electricity industry. Tesla's alternating current (AC) is finally adopted around the world, but Edison goes on to manufacture all kinds of electronic devices (including some of the first light bulbs and record players).

1892 CE Geothermal energy is used to heat buildings for the first time, in Boise, USA.

Thomas Edison

1948 CE The Ghawar oilfield, the largest-known oilfield in the world, is discovered in Saudi Arabia.

1950 CE The world's first nuclear power stations are built in the Soviet Union (an area around modern-day Russia) and the USA.

1980s CE Scientists start to think that burning fossil fuels as a source of energy is harming the environment. A few begin to predict that the climate will change catastrophically as a result.

1. FOSSIL FUELS – TOP BURNERS

Throughout history, humans have burned stuff to create energy. There is no denying that the most popular stuff, from a burning-things-for-energy point of view, is fossil fuels. But where do fossil fuels come from?

Fossil fuels = ancient fuels

All fossil fuels are very old. Fossil fuels began to form underground hundreds of millions of years ago. As a comparison, the stone circle Stonehenge, which most people think is *really* old, was built about 4500 years ago. The first humans only appeared 1–2 million years ago. In fact, when fossil fuels started to be formed, there were still dinosaurs wandering around.

In theory, more fossil fuels could be created – but it would take hundreds of millions of years. Because we cannot wait for them to be replaced, fossil fuels are described as 'non-renewable'.

If fossil fuels such as petrol run out, it will be a very long wait before drivers can fill their tanks again.

Don't worry – we should have more in about 300 million years.

BUZZWORDS!

'Peak oil' is the name for the moment when the amount of oil we extract reaches its maximum. After this, less oil will be pumped each year.

Most estimates of the 'peak oil' moment say it will be pre-2020. Some experts say it has already happened.

How it works: Recipe for fossil fuel

Ingredients

- Dead plants or animals
- Heat and very high pressure
- Hundreds of millions of years

Processes

For oil and gas, use dead marine plants and animals that have sunk to the bottom of the ocean. Bury under layer upon layer of **silt**. Squash. Wait a long time. Drill down. Normally you will have made oil, but if it was really hot down there, you might have made gas instead.

For coal, use dead trees and plants. Pile them high. Bury under tonnes of rock. Wait a few hundred million years. Dig down. Hey presto – coal!

Since the 1700s, coal – the long-dead, squashed-down remains of trees and plants – has been one of our most important energy sources.

What happens when you burn fossil fuels?

When you set light to a fossil fuel, a chemical reaction begins. The fuel combines with oxygen from the air and then energy, water and a gas called carbon dioxide (CO_2) are released.

Burning natural gas produces the fewest chemical **by-products**. Oil and coal both produce additional gases, such as sulphur dioxide.

One side effect of burning certain fossil fuels is acid rain. Sulphur dioxide combines with water in clouds. When it rains, the water is acidic and it damages trees, plants and buildings.

Carbon: It gets EVERYWHERE!

Carbon is a chemical **element**. Carbon combines with more chemical elements than any other element. In fact, carbon is so good at mixing that it is present in every single living thing on Earth.

Plants and carbon

Plants are full of carbon. In fact, they are nearly half carbon. They take in CO_2, which is one part carbon to two parts oxygen. The carbon becomes part of the plant, and the oxygen is released. (This is excellent for humans and other animals which need to breathe oxygen to survive.) What all this means is that the world's plants are a great storehouse for carbon.

Fossil fuels – carbon storehouses

Because fossil fuels are made from lots of plants which have been squashed together, they are a super-concentrated storehouse of carbon.

When you set light to a fossil fuel, the carbon stored inside it joins with oxygen **atoms** and it becomes CO_2 in the air once more.

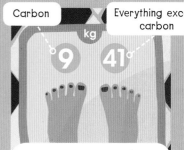

| Carbon | | Everything exc carbon |

There is quite a lot of carbon in humans: if you weighed 50 kilograms, 9 kilograms of you would be pure carbon.

It takes a 10-metre-high pile of dead plants to make a 1-metre-thick pile of coal.

Fossil fuels and CO_2

This table shows how much energy each fossil fuel typically contains and how much CO_2 each produces when burned.

Fuel	Energy content: kilojoules per gram (kJ/g)	Milligrams of CO_2 produced per kilojoule when burned (mg/kJ)
Natural gas	52	53
Oil	43	71
Coal	24	93

Note: A kilojoule is a unit of energy.

FACT FILE

Diary of a carbon atom

Day 1 I'm seeing so many wonderful sights as I float along in the air. The wind has been blowing me (and my friends, the oxygen atoms) all over the place.

Day 9 We were blowing through the forest when I got sucked into a plant. My oxygen mates have abandoned me! Even worse, I seem to have become part of one of the plant's cells. And the view is ... well, there's no view!

Day 27 Just when I thought things couldn't get any worse, my plant has been buried in a mudslide. It is now very dark.

One year later Still dark.

One hundred million years later
Still dark. Also getting a bit squashed down here. And hot. It feels like there are tonnes of rock pressing down on me!

Three hundred million years later
Daylight! I'd been hearing digging noises for ages. Then at last I was loaded onto a cart and ferried to a huge building. I seem to be part of a lump of coal now. Wonder what's next!

One day later Wow, that was hot! The coal was shovelled into a giant, red-hot room. My lump of coal got really hot and vaporized. I floated up into the sky again – at last!

Living in a greenhouse

The gases that are produced when we burn things have a key effect: some of them rise up into the atmosphere where they join lots of other greenhouse gases.

Q: How can a gas be a greenhouse?
A: It cannot, obviously – greenhouses are made of glass and metal, not gas. But greenhouse gases *act* like a greenhouse, causing what is known as the 'greenhouse effect'. They trap heat in Earth's atmosphere, just as panes of glass in a greenhouse trap the warmth of the sun.

Q: I like to be warm – surely greenhouse gases are a good thing?
A: Yes, they *have* been for millions of years: greenhouse gases have been stopping some of our heat from escaping into space, and the warmth they trap is what allowed life on Earth to develop.

Personally, I can't see what all the fuss is about.

Q: So what is all the fuss about?
A: The thing about greenhouse gases is, you need just the right amount to keep the temperature in balance. If there's an excess of greenhouse gases, more heat than is needed gets trapped. This is called the 'enhanced greenhouse effect' – and it might *sound* like a good thing, but it is actually having disastrous effects. (Discover more about these on page 14.)

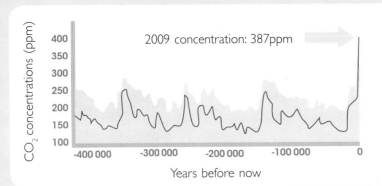

2009 concentration: 387ppm

CO_2 concentrations (ppm): 400, 350, 300, 250, 200, 150, 100

Years before now: -400 000, -300 000, -200 000, -100 000, 0

The red line shows the average temperature in Antarctica, while the blue shows the amount of CO_2 in the atmosphere. The rise in temperature due to increased greenhouse gases is called 'global warming'.

Main greenhouse gases

- *Carbon dioxide*: Probably the most important greenhouse gas at the moment, which has caused 60 per cent of the enhanced greenhouse effect.
- *Methane*: Another important greenhouse gas. There is less of it than CO_2, but it is 20 times more effective at warming the atmosphere.
- *Nitrous oxide*: If you thought methane sounded bad, nitrous oxide is up to 300 times more effective at warming the atmosphere than CO_2, and stays there for 150 years. Fortunately, there is not much nitrous oxide about.
- *Halocarbons*: These are between 3000 and 13 000 times better than CO_2 at trapping heat, and some halocarbons hang around for 400 years.
- *Water vapour*: The amount of water vapour in the air depends on temperature: there is very little vapour over cold regions, and lots in warmer regions. If temperatures rise, the amount of water vapour will increase, making the greenhouse effect even more powerful.

How it works: Cow burps and the end of civilization

A lot of methane is created by cows, who are *constantly* burping it out. Because humans are eating more meat than ever, there are now over 260 million cows in the world. Each burps out several hundred litres of methane a day – so cows are playing a big part in the greenhouse effect.

I'll have some more fizzy drinks, please.

As if you don't burp enough already, Ermintrude!

BUZZWORDS!

Greenhouse-effect deniers (*say* deny-ers) are people who don't accept that humans are causing changes to the greenhouse effect. If you meet one, it is worth pointing out that 97 per cent of the world's climate scientists believe that humans *are* causing an enhanced greenhouse effect.

The effect of global warming

The rise in temperature caused by the enhanced greenhouse effect is called 'global warming'. In human history, global warming has never happened before, so no one is exactly sure what the effects will be. However, it now seems clear that global warming is changing our climate in a way that could have disastrous results for billions of people.

... and the weather used to be *so* predictable at this time of year!

There is a serious point: even if people agree that humans are causing global warming, they don't always want to change their *own* lives by using less fossil fuel.

Temperature statistics

- Between 1900 and 2000, the world's temperature rose by between 0.3°C and 0.6°C. Experts think that by 2100, temperatures in the world's driest regions might rise by as much as 5°C.
- The world's **ice caps** are shrinking. In the Arctic, there is 40 per cent less ice overall than there was in 1980. In the Antarctic, 71 billion tonnes of ice disappeared between 1992 and 2011.
- Since 1992, sea levels have been rising by 0.3 centimetres a year. Experts predict that by 2100, the sea level will have risen by up to 0.59 metres.

FACT FILE

To: All frontline agents
From: Energy Force
Subject: Global warming effects

Some people say that global warming is a matter of opinion. In fact, over a decade ago climate scientists made predictions about what effects global warming would have. Most have come true – some more quickly than in the scientists' worst-case scenarios.

Prediction: Increase in frequency and severity of extreme weather events such as floods and storms.
Has it come true? Yes. Ocean temperature rises caused by global warming have led to an increase in the power and frequency of hurricanes and typhoons.

Prediction: Reduction of sea ice in the North and South poles.
Has it come true? Yes. In the Arctic, the overall amount of ice formed each winter has been getting smaller, and soon there may be none at all during summer. Many **glaciers** around the world are also melting away.

Prediction: Rise in sea levels.
Has it come true? Yes. The combination of rising sea levels and powerful storms has led to flooding around the world.

Prediction: Changes in local climates, with some areas becoming hotter and drier.
Has it come true? Partly. Deserts in the Middle East, Africa, Asia and Australia are all spreading.

Prediction: Changes in deep-ocean currents, which have a direct effect on our weather.
Has it come true? Not yet. For example, predicted changes to North Atlantic currents (which could make Europe and the east side of America up to 5°C colder) have not yet occurred.

What if we do nothing?

No one is completely sure what will happen if the world's temperature keeps rising, but experts have predicted what *might* happen.

Temperature rise	Effect
+1°C	Arctic sea ice disappears in summer; forest fires more common; most coral reefs die; glaciers melt.
+2°C	Amazon rainforest turns into desert and grassland; droughts and heatwaves more common; sea levels rise by up to 7 metres; about 30 per cent of all species are wiped out by habitat loss.
+3°C	Forests disappear; large areas become deserts; farming is difficult so food supplies are low.
+4°C	Melting of Arctic ice releases large amounts of methane and CO_2; sea levels rise by another 5 metres; climate of southern England becomes like that of Morocco.
+5°C	The world is the hottest it has been for 50 million years; Arctic ice disappears forever; coastal cities are abandoned due to flooding; tropical regions become too hot to live in.

BUZZWORDS!

'Carbon trading' is a system for companies, or even countries, to trade their greenhouse-gas **emissions**. Imagine that two companies are each allowed to emit a maximum of 1000 tonnes of carbon each year. One actually emits 908 tonnes, and the other emits 1073 tonnes. The second company buys the first company's 'spare' 92-tonne allowance. Between them, they do not break the emissions limit.

Debate this! Carbon trading

For: It is a good way of controlling overall carbon emissions, and allows poor countries to profit from industries in richer ones.

Against: It is just a way to allow rich countries or companies to buy the right to pollute.

To: All frontline agents
From: Energy Force
Subject: Kyoto Protocol 1997

Politicians have already tried to control global warming using the Kyoto Protocol. This was an international agreement made in 1997, which came into force in 2005. The key terms were:

- Together, the world's countries would reduce carbon emissions to 94.8 per cent of 1990 levels by 2012.
- Many wealthy countries agreed to reduce their carbon emissions to 82 per cent of 1990 levels by 2020.
- Poorer countries did not have limits on their emissions.

Unfortunately, Kyoto did not work. Wealthy countries argued that it was unfair for poorer ones to have no emission targets. The USA, which was the world's biggest CO_2 producer, never implemented the agreement. By 2012, carbon emissions had reached 150 per cent of 1990 levels.

The politicians failed. Now it is up to us to do better!

2. WE DO NOT HAVE TO BURN FOSSIL FUELS TO STAY WARM

Burning the remains of dead plants and animals that are millions of years old is an odd way to get our energy. It only *seems* normal because people are used to it. Once they understand how damaging fossil fuels are, most people want to know if there are alternatives.

Drilling for oil seemed like a good idea at the time ...

Are you *sure* there energy down there

Alternatives to fossil fuels

Some of the alternatives have been around for thousands of years.

- *Solar power:* This turns the sun's rays into useable energy. A simple example is building a house facing the sun, so that the house stays warm. Today, solar panels turn sunlight into electricity.
- *Wind power:* Windmills have been grinding corn for at least 2000 years – but today they are more likely to produce electricity.
- *Water power:* Waterwheels have been providing energy for thousands of years. Today, rivers, waves and the power of tides produce electricity.
- *Biomass energy:* 'Biomass' is any recently living material that can be used as an energy source, such as wood, sawdust or straw.
- *Geothermal power:* 'Geo' means 'from the Earth', and 'thermal' means 'heat', so this type of energy is found underground. Ancient people almost certainly warmed themselves up at hot springs. Today, geothermal energy provides heat and electricity.
- *Nuclear power:* When an atom is split, huge amounts of energy are released. Since the mid-1950s, nuclear energy has been an alternative to fossil fuels.

Together, these are often called 'renewable energy sources'. Unlike fossil fuels, they will never run out.

Back to the future?

No one is sure how prehistoric people might have used energy. Here are some ideas of how they might have used the various sources of energy that were available at the time.

Geothermal heat used in a prehistoric hot tub.

Energy from flowing water used for transportation.

Wind power used for domestic work.

Solar energy used for warmth.

To: Agent U
From: Agent B
Subject: Socrates and the megaron house

Hi U,

A 'megaron house' is designed to trap the sun's heat for warmth in the winter. The first one was designed by Socrates, the Greek philosopher, in about 425 BC.

What makes the alternatives better than fossil fuels?
- They will not run out.
- In general, they do not harm the environment.

Chamber at rear stores heat

Living area

Porch gives summer shade

Floor plan of a megaron house, seen from above.

In summer, the porch stops the high sun shining in, and the house stays cool.

Summer sun

Winter sun

In winter, the sun shines into the house and warms it.

N

Cut-away of a megaron house, seen from the side.

The history of sunshine power

Ever since the first human beings came out of their caves in the morning and sat in the sun to warm up, people have been using solar power. To be fair, it was quite a long time before science came along and made sunshine useful in other ways.

In 1839, a 19-year-old Frenchman named Edmond Becquerel was messing about in his father's laboratory when he discovered a way of turning light, including sunlight, into electricity. Nobody realized the importance of his discovery at the time. It was only later that Edmond became famous for creating the first **photovoltaic (PV) device**.

Another French solar groundbreaker was maths teacher Auguste Mouchout. In 1860, when Europe was going mad for coal, Auguste prophesied that: "Coal will undoubtedly be used up. What will industry do then?"

Auguste decided to build a solar-powered steam engine to solve the problem, and by 1865 he had managed to get one working. Between then and 1914, several inventors developed solar-powered devices – but none were as cheap as coal, so they never became popular.

Solar statistics
- Solar currently provides about 0.7 per cent of the world's energy. This saves 75 million barrels of oil and 35 tonnes of CO_2 per year.
- The amount of power we get from solar energy doubles every year.
- To power the world using solar energy, we would need to cover 0.0005 per cent of the Earth's surface with solar panels.

FACT FILE

Solar power today

In the 1950s, scientists began to develop PV solar cells to provide electricity aboard spacecrafts. The industry grew. Today, lots of **solar farms** are being built and many homes have solar panels on their roofs to heat water.

The electricity that the PV cells produce does not pollute the atmosphere (although manufacturing the cells does cause some pollution). The biggest problem is that, to be efficient, PV cells need lots of bright sunlight, so they do not work well in countries where the weather is often cloudy.

What makes solar energy better than fossil fuels?

- Solar panels do not cause pollution when they produce electricity.
- The source of the energy (sunlight) is free.

Everyday action!

Could you get solar panels at home or school (if you have not already got them)? The government might help with the costs, and some power companies will buy the electricity you produce.

Small, strong PV cells can be used to power all kinds of machines. If it's powered by electricity, it can also be powered by sunlight.

To: All frontline agents
From: Energy Force
Subject: Using solar power

Lots of people think that solar power is complicated, expensive or both. It does not have to be. The two attached articles show good examples of solar energy being used in poorer communities.

SOLAR LIFESAVERS IN AFRICA

In Africa, almost half a million people a year die as a result of breathing in fumes from **kerosene** lamps. Breathing in the fumes can be as bad as smoking 170 cigarettes a year. However, in rural areas without electricity, people have had no choice – until now.

Today, many villagers are using solar lamps as lights. The lamps have small PV cells on top. They just need to be left in the sun, and after dark they provide light for reading, studying and socializing.

Villagers also save money on kerosene: almost $100 a year, which is a lot in a poor country. That money can be spent on food, healthcare and children's education instead.

Since kerosene releases a similar amount of CO_2 to petrol in a car, the new solar lamps are also helping the environment.

The solar ovens saving India's forests

In poor communities in rural India, a quiet revolution is happening. It involves the simplest energy source: sunshine.

For centuries people here have been cooking on wood fires. This has resulted in **deforestation**, which allows the soil to be blown away by wind or washed away by rain. In some areas it has become difficult to grow crops.

Now, young women are being trained to use solar ovens instead of wood fires. These focus the sun's heat into a lined box, which can reach temperatures of over 150°C. That is hot enough for cooking, although it does take longer than it would over a fire.

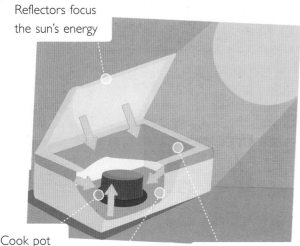

Reflectors focus the sun's energy

Cook pot

Insulated sides and floor

Glass or plastic cover keeps in heat

For the women who use them, there are big advantages to the solar ovens:

- No more time spent scrubbing fire-blackened pots.
- No need to spend hours each day looking for firewood.
- No risk of children falling into a fire and being burned.

What makes the solar ovens better than firewood?

- The carbon stored in the trees' structure gets to stay where it is, instead of being released into the atmosphere.
- Because fewer trees are cut down for fuel, the trees' roots anchor the soil in place, which means that crops grow better.

The power of moving air

For thousands of years, people have been using the wind to make things rotate. Humans have found all sorts of uses for this – from grinding crops to pumping drinking water from deep below the ground. Wind power has even been used to drain land. Large areas of the Netherlands were reclaimed from the sea using wind power.

Lately, people have also been using wind to generate electricity. Tall towers topped by huge, three-bladed propellers are appearing on high ground in many parts of the world. This is where they have the best chance of undisturbed wind flow. These 'wind **turbines**' are usually in groups, which are called 'wind farms'.

Solar and wind energy often work well alongside one another. This is because, during high pressure weather, the clouds are kept away, which allows the sun to shine. During times of low pressure, the sun often doesn't shine, but it's usually windy. Whatever the weather, if you have solar *and* wind power, there should be electricity flowing.

Wind power statistics

Some experts have suggested that wind power could easily provide *all* of the world's energy needs.

- Wind power is the fastest-growing source of electricity in the world.
- A single wind turbine can produce enough electricity for 500 homes.
- One **megawatt** of wind-energy electricity produces 2600 tonnes less CO_2 than one megawatt of fossil-fuel electricity.

FACT FILE

Debate this! Wind turbines

For:
- Once the turbine is built, it does not produce greenhouse gases.
- Turbines only take up a small plot of land, but they produce a lot of energy.

Against:
- Wind turbines look ugly and spoil the view for people who live in the countryside.
- They are noisy.
- They affect wildlife, in particular birds, which can be killed by the turbine blades.
- They are unreliable because the wind does not always blow.

If you lived in a village near a wind farm, how would you feel about it? Do you think you would feel the same way if you lived in a town 50 kilometres away?

What makes wind turbines better than fossil fuels?
- Producing electricity using wind does not cause air pollution.
- The wind is free and will not run out.

Water power 1: Hydro

If you have ever been white-water rafting, you will know how much energy there is in water flowing downhill. Even trying to swim or paddle against the flow of a slow river quickly tires you out.

It does seem an awful lot of effort, dear ...

People have been using 'hydropower', the energy from moving water, for thousands of years. At first it was used in watermills for grinding corn and other crops. Then, in the 1800s, it became possible to use the downhill flow of water to generate electricity. The first hydroelectric power station was built in Northumberland, England, in 1878. The amount of energy it first produced powered just a single lamp.

Within a few years, hydropower had become an important energy source. Today, it provides up to one-fifth of the world's energy, and in 25 countries it produces over 90 per cent of energy. Brazil, Canada, New Zealand, Norway and Switzerland are world leaders in hydropower.

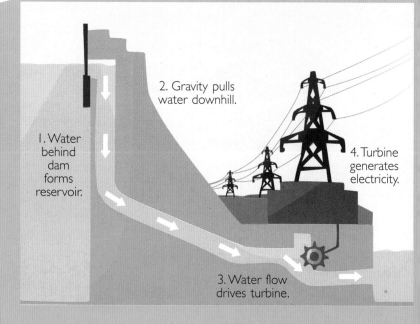

1. Water behind dam forms reservoir.

2. Gravity pulls water downhill.

3. Water flow drives turbine.

4. Turbine generates electricity.

Hydro statistics

- Hydropower is one of the least expensive forms of energy.
- Less than one-third of the world's hydropower potential is currently being used.
- Hydroelectricity is produced roughly ten times more efficiently than electricity from oil-based power stations.

FACT FILE

STOP THE VALLEY VIEW DAM NOW!

Dwr Rhedegog Water wants to dam the river just above Valley View village, creating a huge lake for a hydroelectric power station. Please support the Save Valley View Campaign at the public meeting on Tuesday, where we will raise several objections with the water company:

- It has been proved that hydroelectric reservoirs give off greater greenhouse emissions, in the form of methane, than fossil-fuelled power stations.
- The dam will flood the whole upper valley, destroying the trees and plants that live there.
- The fish that travel to the top of the river to breed will no longer be able to reach their breeding grounds.

In tropical regions, rotting vegetation in the reservoir *can* lead to methane emissions. The problem is easily avoided by clearing vegetation before the area is flooded.

This is true – but global warming is having a much more widespread effect. As long as the trees and plants are not unique, it will still be possible to see examples of them in other places.

Fish ladders have been built at the side of many other dams to solve this problem.

What makes hydropower better than fossil fuels?

- Hydroelectricity is the energy least associated with CO_2 emissions.
- Hydroelectric power stations can be installed anywhere that has a slope and flowing water.

Water power 2: Tidal

Think how difficult it is to carry a full bucket of water more than a few steps. You have to be pretty strong! Now imagine how much energy it takes to propel a small wave across the ocean, or to move so much water that the sea level rises or falls. What if we could use some of that tidal energy instead of burning fossil fuels?

Power from the ocean

People have actually been using energy from ocean tides for hundreds of years. In the 1700s, for example, many mills on the River Thames in England were powered by water that was pushed up the river as the tide rose. Recently, energy from tidal flows has been used to make electricity, and today there are big tidal power projects in Asia, Europe and North America.

Debate this! Tidal power

For:

- Once the power stations are built, they produce cheap electricity.
- They provide power to a wide area.
- Unlike wind farms, they do not spoil people's views.

Against:

- Tidal power stations are expensive to install compared to wind farms.
- They can only be installed in a few places.
- Many fish and other sea creatures are killed by the turbine blades.

This tidal energy plant looks like an underwater wind farm.

Tidal flow makes the turbines spin, which generates electricity.

Cables take the power ashore.

Waves – smashing energy?

Harnessing the power of waves is not easy – the force of the waves often destroys experimental equipment! Another problem is that waves are unpredictable: sometimes they provide too much power, sometimes not enough.

Perfecto!

She's actually riding sunbeams, you know.

How it works: Wave power ... from the sun

Waves are formed when wind blows across the surface of the water. So in a way, wave power is really wind power – except it is not that simple.

Wind occurs when the sun heats an area of land or sea. The air above it rises, drawing in cold air from the sides. So wind energy is actually formed by solar energy!

Sea power statistics

- Up to 80 per cent of the energy in moving tidal water can be harnessed.
- Power generated by La Rance tidal power station in France is one-third cheaper than power from nearby fossil-fuelled power stations.
- Portugal is a world leader in wave power – but even there, less than one per cent of the country's energy comes from wave power.

FACT FILE

What makes tidal power better than fossil fuels?

- Wave power does not produce CO_2 emissions.
- The source of the energy is free.

Biomass – energy from plants and animals

Q: What exactly *is* biomass?

A: Biomass is material that comes from living or recently living things. There are lots of different sources of biomass energy. Some crops can be used as biomass, for example rapeseed can produce oil that is used for biodiesel fuel. Waste from homes, and waste and by-products from agriculture and industry (for example sawdust, waste paper and even sewage) are all types of biomass and can be used as sources of energy.

Biomass statistics

- In 2009, biomass provided 10 per cent of the world's energy.
- Most biomass energy comes from burning wood.
- In 2010, only 1.5 per cent of the world's electricity was generated from biomass.
- For every 6.2 tonnes of CO_2 released by a fossil-fuelled power station, a biomass-fuelled power station releases just 0.8 tonnes.

FACT FILE

How it works: Biomass energy

Biomass can be converted into energy in two ways:

1. *Thermal conversion*

   Thermal conversion uses heat to get energy from biomass. The most obvious example is burning wood. Heat can also be used to warm biomass, producing **flammable** gas and other fuels.

2. *Chemical conversion*

   In a chemical conversion, biomass is turned into energy products without heat. For example, when sewage **decomposes** it gives off methane, which can be used as fuel. And when plants like sugar cane are broken down, they produce a fuel called bioethanol, which can be used instead of petrol.

Q: Why does it all sound a bit like fossil fuels?

A: Well spotted! In fact, fossil fuels were once biomass – and like fossil fuels, biomass gives off greenhouse gases. There is a crucial difference, though: Fossil fuels contain carbon from millions of years ago. This carbon is no longer part of the world's atmosphere. Releasing it by burning the fuel adds to the greenhouse effect. Biomass contains carbon that recently came from the atmosphere. When it is burned, the carbon released just goes back where it came from.

> To: Agent U
> From: Agent C
> Subject: Pineapple power!
>
> Hi U,
>
> Thought you would be interested in this newspaper article. I scanned it from my gran's scrapbook. It is the story of how pineapples used to be grown in places where nature says they shouldn't, using the slow heat of chemical conversion.

What makes biomass better than fossil fuels?

- It makes a much smaller contribution to the greenhouse effect.
- Lots of biomass is waste product anyway.

29th September 1723

Pineapple Delights Guests!

Dinner guests at Nancherrow, home of Sir Dennis Fredericks-Baskerville, were served an astounding treat last Saturday night. They were able to enjoy pieces of what is believed to be the first pineapple ever grown in Cornwall.

The pineapple came from a plant grown in a triumph of scientific **agriculture**, a 'tan pit'. At the bottom is a layer of pebbles, then manure, and finally tanners' bark. This is the crucial ingredient: it is oak bark soaked in water, and gives off constant heat as it slowly rots. It is this heat that makes it possible to grow pineapple plants in Cornwall's sometimes-chilly climate.

Geothermal – the heat beneath your feet

The Earth's inner heat can be used for warmth and generating electricity. Iceland and New Zealand have been using geothermal energy for decades. Both countries have volcanoes, **geysers** and hot springs.

You do not have to live in a volcanic hotspot to take advantage of the Earth's heat. In many parts of the world, the ground not far below the surface stays at a constant temperature. Systems called 'ground-source heat pumps' use this constant temperature to provide buildings with warmth.

How it works: Ground-source heat pump

- Underground pipes are installed about 1.5 metres below the surface. Alternatively, the pipes may go straight down (as far as 100 metres) before returning to the surface.
- The pipes are filled with fluid. This is slowly pumped around, collecting warmth as it travels underground.
- The liquid is used to heat the house, before being pumped back underground to collect more warmth.

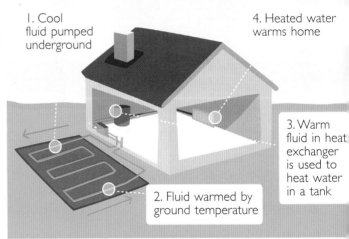

1. Cool fluid pumped underground

4. Heated water warms home

3. Warm fluid in heat exchanger is used to heat water in a tank

2. Fluid warmed by ground temperature

Geothermal statistics

- In 2007, geothermal power produced 0.3 per cent of the world's electricity.
- Experts think that by 2050, geothermal power could provide 3.5 per cent of our electricity and over 4 per cent of our heating.
- For every 1000 homes that install geothermal systems, 2.15 million fewer barrels of oil need to be burned each year.

FACT FILE

2050
0.3%

To: Agent U
From: Agent I
Subject: Geothermal nation

Hi U,

Iceland has been using geothermal energy for years and years – since my grandmother was a little girl. Nine out of every ten houses are heated geothermally, and so is my school. Basically, hot water from under the earth is piped into the buildings to warm them.

After it has been used to warm people's homes, the water is about 35°C. That is a good temperature for melting snow, so some pavements and car parks now have underfloor geothermal heating too.

We also use hot water to drive turbines that make electricity. Hot lakes near power stations are popular swimming spots.

We even use geothermal energy to heat greenhouses. Imagine growing strawberries in Iceland!

What makes geothermal energy better than fossil fuels?

- Using geothermal energy to create heat and generate electricity does not release greenhouse gases.
- Ground-source heat pumps use a small amount of electricity, which can come from a renewable source.

3. TO NUKE OR NOT TO NUKE?

Nuclear power is the new kid on the energy block. It was first developed in the 1950s, and even today only about 30 countries have nuclear power plants. Nuclear energy is very controversial.

What is nuclear energy?

Nuclear energy comes from splitting the nucleus (or core) of uranium or plutonium atoms. These are so small they cannot be seen with the naked eye – but splitting them produces a *huge* amount of energy.

The pros of nuclear energy

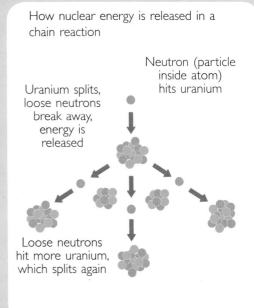

How nuclear energy is released in a chain reaction

Neutron (particle inside atom) hits uranium

Uranium splits, loose neutrons break away, energy is released

Loose neutrons hit more uranium, which splits again

Nuclear power provides plentiful energy with similar levels of greenhouse-gas emissions as wind and hydropower. Supplies of uranium, the fuel for nuclear power, are forecast to last until long after the Sun has burnt out. Nuclear supporters say that it can be managed safely, and that the newest power stations are extremely secure.

Paris, the capital city of France, looks beautiful at night. In 2013, 75 per cent of France's energy came from nuclear power.

FACT FILE

Nuclear statistics

- Nuclear power currently supplies about 12 per cent of the world's energy.
- For every 5g of CO_2 produced by nuclear energy, gas-fired power stations produce 365g and coal-fired stations produce 900g.
- Modern nuclear plants produce power 80 per cent of the time, compared to 35 per cent for wind power.
- Each year, a typical nuclear plant produces about 50 tonnes of waste fuel.

The cons of nuclear energy

There are three main reasons why people object to nuclear energy.

1. It produces dangerous **radioactive** waste that remains harmful for thousands of years. It has to be kept underwater in specially built tanks, surrounded by thick layers of reinforced concrete.
2. There is a history of accidents at nuclear power plants, ranging from small leaks of harmful nuclear radiation to deadly disasters. Find out more on pages 36–37.
3. If you can build a nuclear power station, you might also be able to build a nuclear bomb.

What makes nuclear power better than fossil fuels?
- Producing nuclear energy causes few greenhouse-gas emissions.
- Nuclear power plants are rarely turned off – they run all the time.

To:	Agent U
From:	Agent F
Subject:	Our nuclear neighbour

Hi U,

As well as being an Energy Force agent, I live in a house right beside the nuclear power station at Dungeness in the UK. People often make jokes about it (like, am I sick of catching three-eyed fish?). But we like living here!

It's quiet, apart from the hum of the power station; our rent is *super* cheap because not many people want to live here; and the warm water the station discharges actually does make it really good for fishing.

I'm not sure about the environmental costs of building more of them, though …

Debate this! Nuclear power stations
Would you want to live next door to a nuclear power station, like Agent F? If not, should anyone have to do so?

To: All frontline agents
From: Energy Force
Subject: Going nuclear

Nuclear power is a complex issue. It can provide low-emission energy for millions of people, but some of the radioactive waste it produces will remain a danger for thousands of years.

There is also a risk of nuclear disasters. The attached documents show how the accidents are classified and describe the four worst nuclear accidents in history.

How it works: The IAEA disaster scale

The International Atomic Energy Agency (IAEA) has a seven-stage scale for ranking nuclear accidents. Each level on the scale is roughly ten times as serious as the previous one.

7: accident with widespread health and environmental effects — **7**

6: serious accident with large amounts of escaped radioactivity — **6**

5: several deaths and wider effects on the environment — **5**

4: accident causing at least one death — **4**

3: incident involving 10× the safe level of radiation exposure — **3**

2: minor exposure to radiation — **2**

1: minor equipment problem — **1**

ACCIDENT

INCIDENT

The four worst nuclear accidents in history

1. *Location:*
Chernobyl,
Ukraine
Year: 1986
*IAEA accident
level:* 7

During an experiment that went badly wrong, one of the **nuclear reactors** at the Chernobyl power plant blew up. Within weeks, 30 people had died of radiation poisoning. The World Health Organization estimates that up to 9000 people will eventually die as a result of the accident.

2. *Location:*
Fukushima, Japan
Year: 2011
*IAEA accident
level:* 7

An earthquake and tsunami damaged the nuclear plant at Fukushima, forcing the authorities to evacuate about 300 000 people. Radiation leaked into the local environment and into the sea. A month after the accident, traces of the radioactivity had reached all of the world's oceans.

3. *Location:*
Kyshtym, Russia
Year: 1957
*IAEA accident
level:* 6

An explosion at a nuclear plant in Russia led to reports that radiation poisoning was causing people's skin to fall off. Tonnes of radioactive material spread through the local area. About 200 people are thought to have died after developing cancer as a result of the accident.

4. *Location:*
Windscale, UK
Year: 1957
*IAEA accident
level:* 5

The first nuclear plant to be built in the UK caught fire, spreading radioactive waste throughout the neighbouring environment. Local farmers were banned from selling their goods, and about 100 people are thought to have died from cancer caused by the radioactivity.

4. SMART ENERGY USE

Imagine how your grandmother would have felt when she was a girl if someone had told her that she would one day be sending messages and photos around the world in seconds – using a wireless telephone. Freaked out! But the world we live in is constantly changing because of technology – and technology can help us use energy in a smarter way.

Q: Why is it important to be more careful about how we use energy?
A: It is important to use energy in a smarter way because, as well as developing renewable energy sources, we have to find ways for each person to use less energy. This is urgent – the world's population is growing fast, and at the moment each person is using more energy than they did in the past, not less!

The number of people is steadily overtaking the world's ability to provide enough resources for everyone.

Debate this! How many children?
Would it be right to limit the number of children people can have as a way of helping to solve our energy problems?

Not sure how much more of this I can take ...

BUZZWORDS!

When people talk about 'energy efficiency', they are describing how much energy something requires.

Good energy efficiency = uses little energy

Bad energy efficiency = uses a lot of energy

Anything from a light bulb to a building can be rated for its energy efficiency.

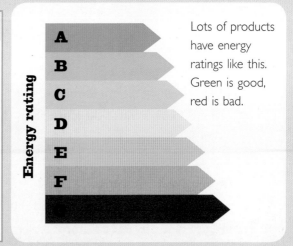

Lots of products have energy ratings like this. Green is good, red is bad.

Q: How can technology help?

A: Technology is already helping the world to develop renewable sources of energy. The trouble is, not many of us can install wind turbines, hydro plants, solar farms or tidal energy plants at home. We have to rely on governments and big power companies to develop those.

The good news is that, when it comes to using less energy, there is a lot that people can do. Every year, we are developing new ways of saving energy. At home, at school, in making or growing the food we eat, in the way we travel, in the buildings we live and work in, and even in the clothes we wear – in every part of our lives, we can be smarter about how much energy we use.

Everyday action!
Energy assessment

Make a list of all the ways you use energy in a normal week. Include not only obvious things, like switching on a light, but also more complicated ones, like eating food that is grown and transported using energy.

Here are some ideas to get you started:
- Charging phone
- Playing computer games
- Watching TV
- Travelling (by road, rail or air)
- Eating (growing and transporting food)
- Clothing (manufacturing and transport)
- Heating and lighting (at home and school)

FACT FILE

Transport statistics

- In the European Union, transport is responsible for about 25 per cent of all greenhouse-gas emissions.
- About 25 per cent of car journeys in the UK are less than 3.2 kilometres.
- Between 1990 and 2013, Australia's transport emissions rose by 53.5 per cent.
- In the USA, over 80 per cent of journeys by people over 16 are made by car or motorcycle.

As the number of people increases, so does the number of cars.

There are more charging points for electric vehicles every year.

Travelling without (environmental) pain

How did you get to school, sports club, the shops, or your friend's house the last time you went? You probably went in a car at least once. And cars – especially big cars – are not great for the environment. Petrol- and diesel-powered cars chug out lots of CO_2, adding to the greenhouse effect. Worse, they produce an average 25 per cent of their CO_2 while sitting in traffic jams. So they are damaging the environment even when they are not going anywhere!

Q: Electric cars are OK, aren't they?
A: Well, it is true that they do not release CO_2 while driving along. But they run on electricity, and right now we get most of our electricity by burning fossil fuels – which produces greenhouse gases. In the future, when electricity comes from renewable sources, electric cars may be a better idea.

Everyday action!
Keep a note of the distance travelled on each of your car journeys for a week. Could you walk or cycle some of the shorter distances?

Q: Are all vehicles equally bad?

A: No, they are not – some vehicles produce more pollution per kilometre than others. As a rule:

- Big cars with big engines are worse than small cars with small engines.
- Old vehicles are usually worse than modern ones.
- Buses and other vehicles that carry lots of people are usually better than cars with only the driver on board.
- Vehicles without engines (bikes, skateboards, canoes, etc.) are better than anything else!

IN CASE OF RISING CO_2 LEVELS, PLEASE ENTER

BIKE SHOP

When was the last time you saw a bicycle filling up with petrol? Cycling (or walking, or skateboarding) is much better for the planet than driving.

Here are some figures that should help you decide which kind of vehicle is best for a journey of 10 kilometres:

Small, efficient car carrying two people	0.6kg CO_2 per passenger
Large car carrying two people	1.3kg CO_2 per passenger
Bus carrying an average number of passengers	1.3kg CO_2 per passenger
Train carrying an average number of passengers	0.5kg CO_2 per passenger

For longer journeys, pick your vehicle carefully. Travelling between London and Edinburgh would generate 33.4 kilograms of CO_2 per person by train, 70.7 kilograms by bus and 91.7 kilograms by plane.

BUZZWORDS!

'Carbon neutral' means something that takes as much carbon out of the atmosphere as it puts in. One example would be going on a flight (which releases lots of CO_2) but paying for some trees to be planted (which, as they grow, will remove the CO_2 from the atmosphere).

Energy at home

In wealthy countries, about a quarter of the greenhouse gases emitted are a result of energy used in people's homes. The top five energy-suckers in our homes are:

1. Heating and cooling the temperature in the house, which uses about 45–55 per cent of the total energy in the average home.
2. Heating water, which uses 10–20 per cent.
3. Lighting and electronic appliances such as computers, chargers and set-top boxes, which use 10–15 per cent.
4. Cooking, which uses about 5 per cent.
5. Refrigeration, which uses about 3 per cent.

So, the best ways to save energy at home involve finding methods to increase and decrease temperatures without using loads of energy.

BUZZWORDS!

An 'energy footprint' is the amount of energy a person (or thing) uses. Someone who uses a lot of energy has a big footprint; using less energy makes your footprint smaller.

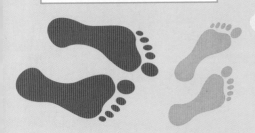

Everyday action! It is curtains for energy wasters

If it is cold but sunny, open curtains or blinds as wide as possible to let in some free solar energy. On hot days, draw the curtains to keep the temperature cooler indoors.

To: Agent U
From: Agent H
Subject: Less power, not more

Hi U,

Here in Germany the government has set targets to use less energy. As a country, we must be using 50 per cent less energy by 2050 than we were using in 2008. By 2050, we plan to be producing 80 per cent of our energy from renewable sources such as wind, solar and water power.

At my school we had a discussion about how we can make this plan work. The result was a checklist, which I have included below. Most of us now use it to monitor our energy use at home.

Please feel free to pass it on to others!

Energy saving at home

If you ...	*Then you should ...*
Turn up the heating when it is chilly.	Put on a sweater instead! A reduction of just 1°C saves about 5 per cent of your total heating energy.
Leave the TV, computer, stereo, etc. on standby.	Turn them off properly, and unplug them if possible. On average, the standby setting uses about 20 per cent of the power used by a device that is fully turned on.
Leave chargers plugged in and on.	Turn off the plug or unplug them. Many chargers still use electricity even when they are not charging anything.
Like to have a hot bath.	Limit yourself: a quick shower uses much less water (which is heated using energy).
Throw clothes in a tumble dryer.	Try drying them on a clothes line in the sun instead. It saves a lot of electricity.

Buildings and energy

There are already lots of buildings in the world, and more are going up all the time. In China, for example, the number of buildings built after 2000 will soon overtake the number built in the thousands of years before. Constructing and using all of these homes, schools and offices takes a lot of energy. Anything we can do to reduce this energy use will help to save the planet.

FACT FILE

Buildings statistics

- Ten per cent of the total energy cost of a house comes from building it. The other 90 per cent comes from heating, cooling and lighting it.
- Worldwide, buildings consume nearly 40 per cent of the world's energy, 25 per cent of its wood, and 15 per cent of its water.
- It is estimated that earth-sheltered homes (homes with earth built up around the outside of the walls) cost 50 per cent less to run than normal houses.

To: Agent U
From: Agent I
Subject: Blowy Hebrides houses!

Hi U,

Winter does get cold up here in the Outer Hebrides, off the coast of Scotland. Sometimes the wind blows so hard that you can barely stand up outside!

We keep our houses as snug as possible. With our wild weather, it is very important to keep the heat in and the cold draughts out. Most people have special thermal **render** on the outer walls, and **insulation** on the inside and in the roof. You can install special doors that stop heat escaping from rooms, ground-source or air-source heat pumps, and windows with three layers of glass to keep warmth in.

Around the world, all sorts of environmentally-friendly buildings have been designed.

Eastgate Centre, Harare, Zimbabwe

Termite mounds inspired this design! Like them, the Eastgate Centre controls the temperature by regulating the flow of air through the building. It has no air conditioning, and uses less than 10 per cent of the electricity that would be required by a building with air conditioning.

Stacking Green, Ho Chi Minh City, Vietnam

The front and back of this house are protected by rows of plants. They shield the inside from hot sunlight, noise and pollution. Air flows through every room, keeping the temperature comfortable without any air conditioning.

Zero-energy houses, Romania

These little houses are built from 97 per cent recyclable materials. They are not connected to outside energy sources. Instead, the houses use solar, hydro and wind energy sources to provide their own power.

Everyday action!

Take a ribbon around your house on a cold or windy day. Dangle it near to the inside edge of each window and door frame. If the ribbon moves, heat is escaping – your parents could save money *and* fight global warming if they can find a way to stop it!

BUZZWORDS!

In environmental speak, a 'green building' is one designed to have minimum impact on the environment. They are sometimes also called 'eco buildings'.

Turn to page 50 to find out about an amazing green school in the UK.

Energy and the things we buy

Every single thing we buy has an energy footprint (see Buzzwords! on page 42). Working out just how big that energy footprint is can be tricky: things that seem similar, such as two jumpers, can have very different-sized footprints. So, what questions do you need to ask to get an idea of how big that footprint is?

Q: How far has it come? And how was it transported?
A: Transporting goods (just as transporting yourself!) generally leads to CO_2 emissions. You might think that the further something has travelled, the bigger its energy footprint will be. Unfortunately, it is not *quite* that simple because not all vehicles have the same environmental impact.

Aircraft	540g of CO_2 for every tonne carried
Lorry	50g of CO_2 for every tonne carried
Ship	21g of CO_2 for every tonne carried
Rail	15g of CO_2 for every tonne carried

To release the same amount of CO_2, something transported by ship would have to travel nearly 26 times as far as something transported by air.

Everyday action!
Check the 'Made in ...' label or sticker next time you buy something, to see if it comes from a long way away. If it does, consider finding a version closer to home to reduce its energy footprint.

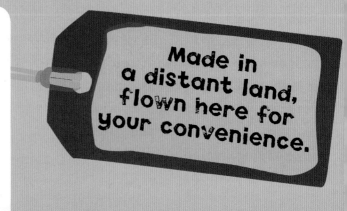

Made in a distant land, flown here for your convenience.

Q: Is it made from recycled materials?

A: Generally, making products from recycled materials uses much less energy than making them from non-recycled ones. Making a recycled can uses 5 per cent of the energy it would take to make a can from scratch. Recycled plastic saves 90 per cent, paper saves 40 per cent, and glass saves 30 per cent.

To: Agent U
From: Agent T
Subject: Recycling crazy!

Hi U,

Some of us here in the USA have gone recycling crazy. All the usual stuff gets separated out into paper, glass, plastic and so on. But I've found out that you can also recycle some surprising things.

- Lots of old clothes can be recycled. There is even a place you can send old bras!
- Your mom and dad's old wine corks (or any other corks) can be recycled into shoe insoles.
- Some companies take back old make-up compacts; a few even give you free make-up if you bring enough old compacts back!
- Old sneakers can be ground down and turned into sports surfaces for running tracks, kids' playgrounds and basketball courts.

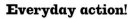

Everyday action!
Check for labels or stickers to tell you if something:
- is made of recycled materials
- can be recycled when you have finished with it.

Food and the wrong kind of greenhouse

There's war, famine and pestilence in the world – and you are worrying about where your peas came from?

Exactly.

Most people know that food is sometimes grown in a greenhouse. The greenhouse keeps plants warm and helps them to grow better than they would outdoors. That is a good kind of greenhouse. Unfortunately, our food is also part of a bad kind of greenhouse – the greenhouse effect. In fact, agriculture as a whole is responsible for up to 33 per cent of our total greenhouse-gas emissions.

Human CO_2 v. fossil CO_2

The CO_2 that humans breathe out is part of *today's* **carbon cycle**, but the CO_2 from fossil fuels was removed from the atmosphere millions of years ago. Burning fossil fuels releases this stored CO_2 back into the atmosphere, and makes the greenhouse effect worse.

Coal contains carbon that is millions of years old.

Humans breathe out carbon that is quite recent.

FACT FILE

To save the planet, we are all going to have to pay more attention to how our food is grown, transported and sold.

Questions to ask your food

Here are some questions to ask your food, when deciding what your next meal is going to be:

- *Are you meat?*

  ... because if you are, it took a lot of energy to get you on the plate. In fact, producing just one kilogram of meat uses the same energy (and CO_2 emissions) as driving a car for 250 kilometres. Vegetables use much less energy.

- *Were you grown using fertilizers?*

  ... because manufacturing **fertilizer** uses a lot of energy, which mostly comes from burning natural gas. Also, fertilizer use has been shown to increase the amount of two greenhouse gases (methane and nitrous oxide) in the atmosphere.

- *Have you come far?*

  ... because if you have, you probably came in a plane. Fresh food that travels a long way is generally transported by air, which uses the most energy and causes the most greenhouse-gas emissions.

- *Are you in season locally?*

  ... because crops that are in season are usually growing naturally outside at the time you buy them. Anything that is not in season has probably been grown in a heated greenhouse – which uses a *lot* of energy.

Debate this! Food from poorer countries

For: The income from food grown in poorer countries helps people in those areas to have a better life.

Against: Transporting fresh food creates a big energy footprint: the food travels by air, which contributes to global warming.

BUZZWORDS!

Organic food is grown without using chemical fertilizers or **pesticides**. Small-scale organic producers usually try to grow food in season, and sell it locally.

BRITAIN'S GREENEST SCHOOL

Howe Dell is a school with a difference. The building is heated by the playground, the roof is covered in plants, the toilets flush with rainwater ... and the desks? The desks are made from old drainpipes.

A tour of the school shows just how different things are here. There is a wind turbine and solar panels for electricity, and solar tubing for hot water. The plant-covered roof provides insulation and a living space for wildlife.

Inside, there are light wells, which are open areas or shafts that allow natural light in. This cuts down the energy needed for electric lighting. The walls are super-thick to keep in heat. The special windows let in light and solar energy, but they stop heat escaping.

The school's biggest green achievement is out of sight, however. Underneath the playground is a system of fluid-filled pipes that gather heat on hot days. The heat is transferred to highly insulated thermal storage. In winter, the stored heat is used to warm the whole school.

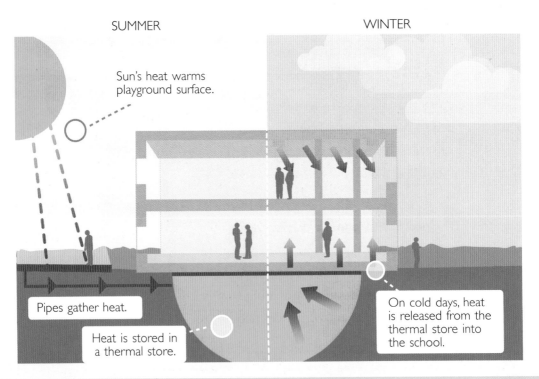

SUMMER

WINTER

Sun's heat warms playground surface.

Pipes gather heat.

Heat is stored in a thermal store.

On cold days, heat is released from the thermal store into the school.

Saving the planet at school

Sadly, not every school can be like Howe Dell – not immediately, anyway.
But there are plenty of things all schools can do. Here are our top five places to start.

1. *Encourage parents not to drive to school*
   Walking is best. How about setting up a 'walking bus', which collects children along the way? Parents know their children are safe, and everyone gets some exercise.

2. *Plant trees in the school grounds*
   Trees remove carbon from the atmosphere while growing. Observing how trees grow is good for science lessons too!

3. *Increase reusables*
   For example, instead of disposable cups, have cups that can be washed and reused. Put food straight into a lunchbox instead of wrapping it in foil or cling film.

4. *Go renewable*
   Some electricity companies offer 'green tariffs'. Many of these work by supplying energy from renewable sources. Others support environmental projects, such as tree planting schemes.

5. *Start a magazine library*
   Printing and transporting magazines costs energy. If you start a library, lots of people can read a single magazine instead of everyone buying their own copy.

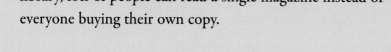

Everyday action!

Campaign for cycle training at school (if there is not any already).
Once parents know their children can cycle safely, they might let them ride to school. You might have to campaign for bike parking too!

5. ENERGY QUIZ

Having read the training manual, you should now be ready to go out and start persuading people to think about their energy use and what it does to the planet.

There is one last task ahead of you, though: the Energy Quiz. Check your score at the bottom of page 53. (Just so you know: not all of the possible answers are completely serious.)

1. *What happens when you burn fossil fuels?*
   a You often find dinosaur bones.
   b You are using a renewable energy source.
   c Carbon that has been stored for millions of years is released back into the atmosphere.

> Watch out for the T-Rex.

2. *What is the 'enhanced greenhouse effect'?*
   a An increase in the number of greenhouses to grow organic food.
   b The cause of tomatoes turning red (because it is so hot in a greenhouse).
   c An increase in greenhouse gases that is leading to a rise in the air temperature, called global warming.

3. *Is CO_2 the only greenhouse gas?*
   a Yes, because it is the only one that contains carbon.
   b No, there are other greenhouse gases – but CO_2 plays the biggest part in the enhanced greenhouse effect.
   c No, providing you keep the greenhouse door open.

4. *What is global warming?*
   a A potential disaster that could spell the end of human life.
   b A good thing, as we will all save on heating bills.
   c The reason bears go into hibernation.

> Can't see what all the fuss is about.

5. *What effect is global warming likely to have on the animal kingdom?*
   a The animals will be fine, except penguins, who will get hot and grumpy.
   b Thousands of species will die out as their native habitats disappear.
   c Animals will be forced to start wearing sunglasses and suncream.

> Not all that keen on coconut, though.

6. *What was the Kyoto Protocol?*

   a   A 1997 attempt by the world's politicians to end global warming.

   b   An almost-complete failure (because carbon emissions have actually increased since it was signed).

   c   Both of the above.

7. *The best way to travel is:*

   a   On foot or using a human-powered vehicle (for example a bike, scooter or skateboard).

   b   By bus or train.

   c   Stretch limo, obviously. Or private jet.

8. *What is the best meal for an Energy Force agent?*

   a   Burger! Always been my favourite.

   b   Breakfast – a good breakfast gets the day off to a solid start.

   c   One made with local, organic ingredients, and without much meat in it.

A fun way to help save the planet!

SCORE YOURSELF:

Give yourself a point for each correct answer.

Over 6 points: Great score, well done! You will be an excellent Energy Force agent.

5 or 6 points: A good try, but it might be worth rereading some bits of this manual again.

Fewer than 6 points: Don't despair! More intensive training might be required, though.

ANSWERS:

1 c; 2 c; 3 b; 4 a; 5 b; 6 c; 7 a; 8 c

Glossary

agriculture: growing crops and breeding animals

atoms: tiny particles that make up every object in the universe

by-products: products created during the process of making something else

carbon cycle: the process of recycling carbon through the atmosphere and all living things

decomposes: breaks down; rots

deforestation: removal of trees (and other plants) from an area

element: the most basic form of matter, which can't be broken down into simpler substances

emissions: the release of something, usually gas, into the air

fertilizer: substance that helps plants to grow faster and/or larger

flammable: capable of being burned

generators: machines for turning movement into electricity

geysers: places where columns of water and steam erupt from the Earth

glaciers: large blocks of compacted snow and ice

harnessed: made use of

ice caps: large plates of ice

insulation: material that stops heat from passing from one space to another

kerosene: fuel made from oil; known as paraffin in some parts of the world

megawatt: unit of power

nuclear reactors: machines used for splitting uranium atoms

pesticides: substances that kill anything which could damage crops, such as insects

photovoltaic (PV) device: device that changes energy from the sun into electrical energy

radioactive: giving off radiation, which is harmful to all living things

render: covering that is added to the outside of stone, brick or other building materials

silt: small pieces of sand, earth or clay

solar farms: groups of panels which turn solar energy into electricity

sustainable energy: energy produced and used in a way that means it will not run out or harm the environment

turbines: machines that produce electricity from the movement of a spinning wheel or blade

vertical axis: a line that runs straight up and down

Index

About the Author

As a boy I spent a lot of time roaming around with my basset hound, Bullet. My mum still complains about the time the police brought us home after we'd gone fishing in someone's goldfish pond! After that, I was strongly encouraged to keep busy doing sports. Today, I still love swimming, surfing (surfing rules!), snowboarding and cycling. Somehow, amongst all the sporting activity, I also found time to go to college.

I actually got the idea for this book while cycling along with my dog, Daisy The One-Eyed Surf Dog (who sits in a basket on the back of my bike, surveying the world like the Queen). We'd just overtaken a line of about 100 cars, all going nowhere with their engines running. 'This is bonkers,' I thought. 'Look at all the pollution. No wonder the planet's in trouble.' I got a bit depressed. Then I thought, 'What if young people ignored the grown-ups, and just got together and started changing things? What kind of stuff would be in their training manual?' This book, I hope, is part of the answer.

Greg Foot, Series Editor

I've loved science ever since the day I took my papier mâché volcano into school. I filled it with far too much baking powder, vinegar and red food colouring, and WHOOSH! I covered the classroom ceiling in red goo. Now I've got the best job in the world: I present TV shows for the BBC, answer kids' science questions on YouTube, and make huge explosions on stage at festivals!

Working on TreeTops inFact has been great fun. There are so many brilliant books, and guess what ... they're all packed full of awesome facts! What's your favourite?